WE ARE BULLETPROOF

SHIZA KARIM

Contents

Contents

Contents

Disclaimer

This anthalogy is a work of fiction.

The compiler has tried her level best to edit the write ups and to provide a error free script. We have ensured that plagiarism content was eliminated. In case of any error or plagiarism detected, neither the compiler nor the publication house is responsible. The co authors solely hold the responsibility of theirs particular content

Acknowledgements

The making of this anthology would not have been possible without our co authors. My hearty gratitude to everyone who has put their heart and soul and have made efforts for this book. I thank my co authors and words of soul publication team who have worked hard to make this book successful and better. A hearty thanks to everyone who supported and participated in my book written about "WE ARE BULLRTPROOF".

Above all, i thank Almighty to give me the strength to complete the book.

About The Book

' We truly have the best fans in the world', 'We are family', 'I want them to be happy... Even happier than we are' 'we're all strong, we'll find a way and 'use me, use BTS to love yourself'.

BTS has always supported and been with army's not just then when they were small, but even then when they crossed the hurdles and became the biggest boyband of the world. They have taught us to be strong, withstand against failure and taught us to love self, respect self and value one self. BTS is not just a boyband but the inspiration and a source of motivation for the whole world. BTS taught ARMYs to enjoy every little thing of life ans has vanished the darkness of millions and billions of life. So does ARMY. They promised to be with them forever and support each one of them equally and made them energetic and full of contentment with their cheers and love.

WE ARE BULLETPROOF is not just an elegant and angeliferous book filled with the utmost emotions but the love, support and proud of 25 global ARMYs along with the compiler for the 7 stars of their life. Everyone in the book has clearly mentioned the true love for bangton boys. Everyone has conveyed their tenderness regarding BANGTONSONEYONDAN through their inked verses of everyone said together
"WE ARE BULLETPROOF".

CHAPTER ONE

COMPILER OF THE BOOK

Hello! SHIZA KARIM from Patna, Bihar. She is a student in 8 standard and is 13 years old. She is a co author of more than 110

anthologies and a compiler of 9 anthologies. Her debut book as a co author is ARMY'S FOREVER based on BTS. She loves to express her thoughts and feelings through her ink verses. Her main write ups were about social issues like drug addiction and abuse and rape, BTS, happiness, sorrows, girl child, has written some inspirational stories and poems and on much topics. She loves music. She is a little girl with big dreams and aims. She is a devotee of Islam.

ARMY'S FOREVER

BTS is not just a name

They aren't working only

To get fame

They aren't bad

They are magnificent

They are making people happy by their

Works and music, well

They faced a lot of struggles, hurdles like hell

Everyone wanted to destroy them

Haters are ready to annoy them

But, BTS is not just a name

They are angels from heaven

You know, they are only seven

But they combined all the world

By their music

Every member has his own charisma

Jin in his own wwh style

Suga in his own swag

Hobi is all with his hope

Jimin with his cute eye smile

Namjoon with a lot of knowledge

Jungkook with his big doe eyes

And V lives in his own world

Where only armys and V exist

They inspire us

To peruse our dreams

Even if no one supports

They teach us

To be real and

Not to coat ourselves with the sheet

That the world want us to be

Even as solo

Each member is master

They call their fans as ARMY

Isn't it astonishing

That each one of their fan

Is strong like an army force

Ready to be by their side

Ready to stan them

Forever and ever

BTS' ARMY and AMRY'S BTS

The never ending bond forever

To walk along

To carry up with BTS

To make them even more successful

To make them feel proud of themselves

This never ending saga that

Every individual ARMY can proudly say that

I AM A BTS ARMY FOREVER.

By SHIZA KARIM

CHAPTER TWO

HARSH KUMAT

Harsh Kumat is a 26 years old young , vibrant and joyful personality who like to spread smile and happiness through his work and words.He is born in Pink City, Jaipur, brought up in Manchester of Rajasthan Bhilwara. He loves to create the music to generate new energy. He is currently working with his father at their family business of Textiles.

MY WELL-WISHERS LOVE ME TRULY

They love me that is why they hold me.

They tell me so I rise, but they never scold me.

They keep me like an open page, they never fold me.

When I am wrong they take the necessary pain to

Correct me.

They have the hyper voltage that charges my battery.

Together when we come we magically grow a tree.

I must be more humble and thankful.

I must close my eyes to feel my spark.

I must be more calm and observant.

To learn it all again from the start.

PATIENCE IS THE KEY

I must do what' is necessary.

To make it bold from blurry.

Just do it quickly, still please don't hurry.

The worries and sadness need to be buried.

Don't keep your heart with a single grudge.

Life is too sweet, have some chocolate fudge.

Celebrate, love work and wisdom sometimes it's amazing not to
judge.

CHAPTER THREE

SAUMYA KINNARI KARTIK DALAL

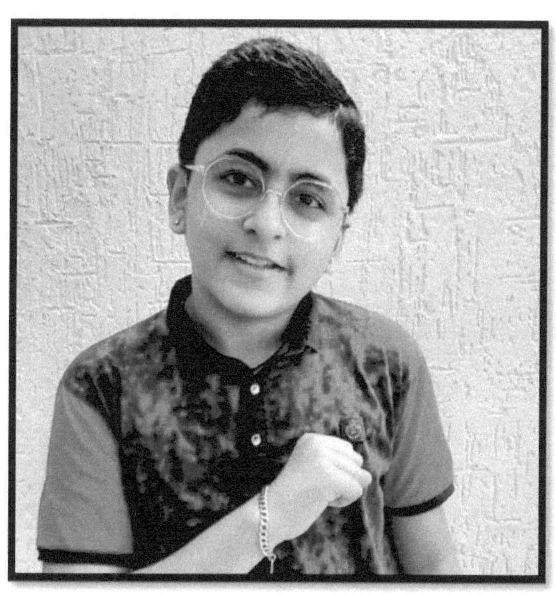

Saumya Kinnari Kartik Dalal is a 13-year-old boy, born in the year 2009, studying in grade 8th at Kapol Vidyanidhi International School ICSE. He lives in a Hindu Gujarati joint family. His loved name is Somu. He likes to write poems. He writes poems in Hindi, Gujarati & English Languages. He has worked as a co-author in more than 125 anthologies. He is also an author of मेरी परछाई मेरी कवतिाएँ, his first solo book. He sees himself in the future as a good poet.

14

BULLETPROOF BTS

' We are Bulletproof' song by none other than BTS was a melodic, symbolic, euphoric, beautiful and nostalgic masterpiece of a song. They were so beautiful in this song. I loved the echo of the voices and the breathy onsets, as they gave it a spacious sound.

Jungkook's falsetto starting off the song was so breathy, beautiful, and touching. My heart was hooked on this song after those first few lines. V's beautiful voice harmonises with his mellow, low and deep voice, sending chills down my spine. J-Hope's melodic, chesty rap came in, which contrasted the falsetto from before. Something I've always loved about BTS is that they have often done this in their songs, and it just always gave me that 'togetherness' feeling, as I think of it as multiple different things coming together. Jin's part was so airy and so pleasing to the ears. The chorus too was breathtaking. Suga's rap afterwards, once again, contrasted the high singing in the chorus. All 7 of them did a fabulous job at conveying the message they were trying to convey. Their clothing was fashionable and it has made a trend among youngsters. Their dance moves and style have already made everyone their fans. Video recording and editing were so sharp that catching mistakes was next to impossible. I don't have much to say except that the lyrics were so BTS, and therefore so wholesome, honest and tearful. Like I was so moved when I read them. They expressed their love for ARMY in such an amazing way and expressed to us how hard they worked to be where they are. BTS has always been my favourite and I am a BTS fan forever.

#Somu Saumya Kinnari Kartik Dalal

CHAPTER FOUR

JOSE ACHSACH ALANKARAM

Jose Achsach Alankaram says " She will never hide her talents, if she is silent she will be forgotten. If she is not advance people will insult and never let her achieve her goals. If she will get scared and walk away from her challenges today she will never be able to face herself . she rejects the stationary position because it is always the beginning at the end. The above philoshophy has played an vital role in shaping her objectives and framing her plans for the future.

18

BTS LOVE MYSELF CAMPAIGN

BTS boy band team conducts the love yourself Campaign. The name of the campaign is coming from their most popular album called LOVE YOURSELF. Everyone may be thinking or they don't know what is the reason behind the Love Myself Campaign or why this campaign is conducted by BTS. The reason is initial period of BTS career as boy band they faced lot of dislikes and bad comments from people such as their singing methodology and some people judged there appearance and character which lead them into anxiety and depression. At this time of period BTS members were thinking to leave the group, also feeling very low some were they thinking to kill them self. That time they need to overcome their depression and anxiety, also they need to face the people who have interest in there songs. After overcoming there anxiety and depression. They think to make songs on there journey of this anxiety and depression. Then they thinked that why can't we make camping which will help people to overcome from anxiety and depression.

Thorough there songs and there speech they started helping people to overcome the problematic situation. At that period of time (2017) United Nations Assembly called BTS to collaborate with them to make young and youth people save from anxiety, depression, and self-killing, abuse. Then it was successfully happing in South Korea and also overall the world.

Now it has been a UNICEF partner since 2017, shared a virtual message vowing to continue the LOVE MYSELF campaign for love and unity, especially in times of social isolation.

As part of a new global partnership, BTS and Big Hit will donate more than $ 1 million to UNICEF, along with a portion of the proceeds from the sale of LOVE MYSELF products and the proceeds from the sale of the LOVE YOURSELF album.

"We are very impressed and grateful that the LOVE MYSELF campaign, which started from a small step, has now been expanded into a larger partnership, and we have been striving for" LOVE "on our own. I think I've grown as a team and as an individual, "said band member RM.

Due to school closures, physical distance measurements, and reduced access to services, the COVID-19 pandemic is the psychological psychological nature of children and adolescents, especially those who may be at risk of neglect. Helped to shed light on the importance of social well-being, both online and offline abuse, and bullying. UNICEF is responding to these changing times with a rejuvenated strategy to protect and promote the well-being of all children and adolescents around the world.

"COVID 19 has caused enormous damage to all of our lives and emotional well-being, especially children and adolescents," said UNICEF Executive Director Henrietta Fore. "Through their music and message, BTS said to their worldwide audience,' You are not alone. This is a difficult time for all of us. And together, with love and kindness, we. Will overcome this. "As our partnership enters a new phase, we are working together to reinvent a world that is kinder, safer, and more connected. "

Since 2017, BTS and Big Hit's LOVE MYSELF campaign has raised $ 2.98 million worldwide for UNICEF's efforts to end violence against children and adolescents, and young people around the world begin to talk about their experiences. Have helped. As a UNICEF supporter, BTS will meet with world leaders and world leaders at the UN General Assembly's annual meeting in New York to promote UNICEF's campaign for love and kindness online and in real life. We have released an exclusive music video to help. Special stands at concert venues around the world provide information on how individuals can protect themselves and each other from violence and bullying.

UNICEF and its partners strive to ensure that all children have a loving, compassionate, safe and supportive relationship at home, school, and community, and access to quality mental health and mental health support services.

Children and teens have the right to pursue their lives in safety and happiness and to grow with love and care. At this very moment, however, some of them are falling victim to various levels of violence. Many of them are unable to enjoy their fair share of chances to dream of a healthy future.

"Love myself, share the love"—this is the true meaning of love and what we want to share with others and promote in the broader world. We want to lend a helping hand to children and teens exposed to violence. With our love and care, this world can be turned into a better place where people can dream of tomorrow."

AKINLUYI OLUWATOMISIN ADETAYO

She's Akinluyi Oluwatomisin Adetayo she's 16 she's a Nigerian she's a secondary school student she loves writing a lot and she's so glad to be a co-author in this anthology.

24

Mmmm BTS

A group of 7army with unique ~ different characters.

A group of 7men that pulls crowd and attention of over 1000people.

A group of 7which names are;V,Jimin,J-Hope,Jungkook,RM,Jin and suga,mmmm wow a mysterious 7.

BTS are one of the first award winning K-pop singers.

They are always willing to help the A.R.M.Y. and frequently express their admiration for the fans.

The fact that BTS is so sincere and genuine is the main reason I think they're remarkable.

The South Korean boy band BTS

The South Korean boy band BTS, short for Bangtan Sonyeondan or Beyond the Scene, has been killing it in the music industry since their debut in June of 2013.

V, Suga, Jimin, Jungkook, RM, Jin, and J-hope make up the South Korean boy band BTS, which has seven members. BTS is one of the most successful K-pop groups in the world and was one of the first to do so.Amazing riiii

A group that features lots of talent and strong suits.

The group.

BTS members RM, Jin, Suga, J-Hope, Jimin, V, and Jungkook all have distinct characteristics, which I believe contribute to why they are so popular with fans.

NEELAKSH OJHA

Neelaksh is a good soul which truly tries hard to make u smile.

BTS ARMY'S

Bangtan Boys, is a South Korean boy band that was formed in 2010 and debuted in 2013 under Big Hit Entertainment. The septet—consisting of members Jin, Suga, J-Hope, RM, Jimin, V, and Jungkook—co-writes and co-produces much of their own output. Originally a hip hop group, their musical style has evolved to include a wide range of genres.The band was there to meet US president Joe Biden to discuss about the rising cases of hate crimes against South Asians. Much to their surprise, Joe Biden playing their song 'Butter' to make them feel at home. Singer Charlier Puth let the cat out of the bag as he confirmed his collaboration with K-pop group BTS.

Bts is kpop boy band from BigHit Entertainment.Bts means Bulletproof Boyscoucts in korean but they have recently changes their english name to Beyond the Scene.They have seven members (3 rappers and 4 vocalists) and debuted on June 12th, 2013.

Kim Namjoon

Jin

Suga

J-Hope

Jimin

V

CHAPTER SEVEN

VIMALA THANGGAVILO

T. Vimala is the youngest daughter of Mr. & Mrs.
S.Thanggavilo M.Thevanai. She was born and lives in Malaysia.
Written more than 200 quotes and poems. Co-Author for over
30 anthologies. We are grateful for everyone's support. Thank

you.
Instagram @fun_luv_joy and @uninterruptible_quotes

IMPRESSED

Magical voice your throne,

Music is a skyscraper,

In the song,

You are My Universe,

Has touched millions of your fans,

All the singer is not from a fairy tale,

Found the dedication,

In every soul,

As all the words sang is soulful,

Vibe us from the sore.

Keep locking with creation,

Serve us with more satisfaction,

Throughout the journey,

Gonna be levitation.

Kamsahamnida, BTS Band!

SOOTHING

Crispy music tempering soul,

Echoes filled the room of heart,

Every beat rhythmically enforces,

Fame is not from the frame,

As you have a lot of dreams,

Everyone on your team,

Having a mind melted voice,

It makes all changeover,

The one look unfamiliar,

To be more familiar,

Have tons of fans,

All over the world,

Remote emotionally,

From your BTS band tremendously.

Arasso...

TAPASWINI MOHANTY

Tapaswini Mohanty is a student of class VI is a accomplished author and co-author who has worked in many anthologies and is currently learning Korean language along with Japanese and is fluent in English language. She is also a photographer and artist.

YOU CAN FIND HER CONTENT
INSTA ID : tapaswini_mohanty1

YOUR EXISTENCE IS MY HEART BEAT

Your Existence makes me feel special,

That I'm not alone,

In this cruel and selfish world you held my hand like no other,

Like I'm the moon and you're my light,

Without light moon is nothing,

Like that without you I am nothing,

You're with me all the times I cried,

You took me when I was abandoned by others,

Loving you was my best decision,

Promise me that you will never left me abandoned,

I always pray for you,

To with me always,

I want to be an army forever,

Always the precious bond we share forever,

BTS and ARMY forever,

You're my pain and my relief also,

You're my morning and evening,

You're my light and my destiny,

You're my love,

The proof of my existence.

BANGTAN PAVED THE WAY

You're my love my last breath,

Even though I am not with you but always with you,

You saved us from depression,

You taught us how to love ourselves,

People said, you're nothing you can't do anything,

But today you proved that teamwork makes the dreamwork,

The music which inspires millions of people,

With such a deep meaning in it,

We knew that loving you was not a mistake,

And we'll not regret for our whole life.

CHARMILA YERRA

Charmila hails from a small town in Visakhapatnam. She is an ex-Software professional and an ex-Hr professional.Writer and an artist by passion. Charmila's love for literature, art and passion for writing made her pen down her amazing debut fictional book 'The Darkness In Her Life'. Her thoughts in the story would make you feel like the characters inside. She has

co-authored 38 anthologies so far.

DEAR K-POP

Itwas on a fine day,

I came to know you

Not one but you Seven

Yes you are the heaven

I was on a ride but struck

It was you seven who stopped

But I didn't notice much

As I was hooked up to your bunch

I adored your inner soul

Much than the outer depositions

Yet I don't understand

After all why I got addicted.

I FELT

It was on the day I felt

You are the wonder seven

Who leave us all in heaven

Every concert you make

I am not be beautiful

I am not be like you

I am not be wealthy to reach you

But I always have eyes on you

True but weird I love you

Yes but guilty to be unknown to you

Real but sad that I can't reach you

Well although I have my heart for you.

CHAPTER TEN

DEYA RAJIV MUKHERJEE

She is Deya Rajiv Mukherjee, a girl from West Bengal, India. She is currently a graduation student of 6th semester. She is a student of South Calcutta Girls' College, Kolkata and her Honours subject is Sociology Honours. She is an army and really loves BTS ?. Her hobbies include listening to music and writing. She is also a co – author in many anthologies.

52

BTS IS THE MOST FAMOUS K-POP

BTS, is the most famous K- Pop band in the world right now. This year will mark the 9th anniversary of the band on June 13, 2022 from their debut date which is June 13, 2013. From the beginning, they had to face a lot of issues

Such as hate , racism and also many struggles.

But now , their hardwork has paid off finally. They have made a huge number of records as Korean band. Today, they enjoy a huge fan base

And extreme popularity from their fans, who are known as army , in all corners of the world.

As an army, I am really proud of them and their achievements. I will always support them till the end. Their music is a comfort zone and a mental healer to millions of army's, including me. For me personally also, when I lost my dad in 2018, I was literally very upset and couldn't find hope , inspite of the fact that everyone tried their best to console me. But one day, I found BTS. Their songs gave me hope and confidence. They have taught me many things such as how to love myself, how to work hard, how to always follow my dream , don't care about what other people say. Still now, they are my magic shop.

If I ever get a chance to meet them , I would say thank you for everything they did . I don't know whether I will be able to go to their concert, but I will be there till the end for then and this is for sure .

I hope that they continue to rise and shine brightly like this and have a bright future ahead.

Always remember that you are not alone , a large number of army's are there for you. Our bond is very strong and nothing can break it. Army and BTS will always stay together.

Lastly, a very happy 9th anniversary BTS ?. Wishing you lots of good wishes for your career ahead . Take care, stay safe and healthy. Love you so much...

Borahae ?

SAANIKA DINKAR SATHE

Her name is saanika dinkar sathe

She is a pharmacist by qualification.
She loves to write because
it is away to express our feelings in words.

56

WHAT A RELIEF

what a relief it's already been 5 years since we debuted; just boys with many dreams. We had nothing,

but we have many things now. We were only dreaming, we dreamed about flying high up in the sky but it's too high and cold, it's hard to catch our breath.

But we became the dream of someone. Life is full of choices and regrets – I'm scared, and so are we.

The brighter the light on us, the darker the shadow.

But what a relief that we have 7 members; what a relief that we have each other.

MY DEAREST BTS

The live of my life,

My spark for inspiration

And my confidence for passion.

7 Korean men, Influencers of all these thing and so much more.

Worthy of the world and it's love within it, Making many souls sing to their glowing rhythm.

Suga with his rap and RM with his flow. J-hope with his joy and Jimin with his tiny toes.

V with his heart and Jungkook with his voice.

Jin with his beautiful face everyone knows.

CHAPTER TWELVE

MARIAM OREOLUWA ARIWOOLA

Mariam Oreoluwa Ariwoola is a Nigerian poet and a writer. She is a student and a young lady aspiring to change the world with her writing. She's look forward to touching hearts of many. She's participated in many anthologies and written many poems of her own. She goes by the pen name Maryam inks.

HIS VOICE

Without a drummer drumming

Without a singer singing

But only his heard voice

I go crazy hearing him talk

Like a song , I sing to his voice

Like a drum , I give beat to his voice

Like a dancer, I dance to it

So sweet, sonorous, pleasant to the ear

I must say it's so melodious

Not only that, like food,so yummy

Oh I hope I hear this always, forever

He shall stay and not leave me

He gingers my body and soul

Which all seemed liveless

He turned it into lively body for me

Voices are souls lifter

But some are mood spoiler

The hearing of some gladdens you

While some saddens you

Life is such an irony

Always saying opposite of things

Why not be a soul comforter

Stop being a voice irritant

Be people's source of happiness

People's source of contentment.

Maryam inks.

EYE SORE

Part of the body attract people

So appearance talks more of you

Some are not worth looking at

Some are being looked forward to be

Oh life is indeed,a choice

The physique of humans

Is special in all kinds

As no human mould human

All is made by God

But some remoulded themselves

Giving themselves what HE didn't give them

Making it an eyesore to people

Thing of disgust , which is made well by him

In the name of fashion,head is disturbed,tempered with

Nose disfigured, eyes with holes

Oh so uninteresting saying by mouth

All part of the body are beauties granted unto you by God

Why turn it into an irritating body.

For every crime is punishment

One also to be melted out

To the ones who calls God incapable

Why didn't they make themselves

If capable enough, shouldn't have depended on HIM

There's punishment as they have called him a liar.

Maryam inks.

CHAPTER THIRTEEN

ALINA MOHANTY

ALINA MOHANTY, doctor in making and author in progress. She is two times Record Holder. She has been part of 200+ anthologies. She is the author of "A CUP OF SOCIETY". Apart from this, she is a dancer, singer, painter and tarot reader. She is an animal lover and also an bibliophile.

CHAPTER FOURTEEN

ICONIC

Bangtan boys,
Are treat to soul and eyes.
These pretty face have mellifluous voice.
And they are iconic of people's choice.
Every song of there is dynamite.
They are like my music of every night.
Indeed they are star ,
Star of elixir.
So soothing and peaceful,
Group of seven
They are like Angels from heaven.
Praises and applause turns mere
When these guys are supremely rare.
What makes them more attractive,
Is their way of being productive
And the way they love each other.
For a band it's a must gesture.
They are rulling heart
And they will be forever doing that.
For every time a band come.
They will consider BTS as their exemplar.

PURPLE

Look at these septet,

Their song is a burning climax.

Soothing and inspiring

BTS is simply an iconic Army.

They say ," I purple you".

So do we

The heartthrob boys are divine,

The way they hold together

Are examples of true friends.

We learnt to love from them

And we love them.

They hold again our broken part,

They inspire us to work hard,

They sparkles us to love more.

They are our source.

Source of joy,love and light.

These boys are treat to sight.

So now that anyone ask,

"Who do you love ?"

I say ,"it's Bangton Boys."

CHAHAK KAKWANI

Chahak is a student of 12th and she loves to write because she thinks penning down her feelings is the most beautiful way of expressing herself. She has other hobbies like dancing as well. She's from Kota, Rajasthan. She is an ARMY.

WE ARE BULLETPROOF

In my dark times you were my HOME,

You were the magic to my MAGIC SHOP,

I NEED YOU because

You are the cause of my EUPHORIA,

Your music is the DNA in my veins,

And BUTTER gave me PERMISSION TO DANCE,

Cause this is not FAKE LOVE,

You are a DYNAMITE to the world,

You got this SPRING DAY coz

You gave your BLOOD SWEAT & TEARS.

Thankyou for showing me the BEST OF ME.

DON'T LEAVE ME ever,

Coz you are my BOY WITH LUV.

Grateful for the fact that you and your music taught me that there is TOMORROW, a new day always, and my best is YET TO COME

Because LIFE GOES ON.

Lot's of love BTS

WE ARE BULLETPROOF ♡.

CHAPTER SIXTEEN

BLESSY A . CARLIN

Blessy A. Carlin is a passionate and aspiring writer, and is currently pursuing International Business from Commerce branch. She loves to accept new and challenging tasks. Being a voracious reader, she started to attempt using her intellectual mind to express her thoughts by penning down on blank papers.

She believes that a pen in hand and an artistic mind will give a whole new perspective to the same old world. As of now she is trying to figure out her future path in the darkness of this crucial world using anthology as her sparkling glimmer, "Words give expression to her emotions, soul to her skills and hope to her future".

BTS SONG

Smooth like Butter, living a life filled with BTS songs,

Yeah, Life goes on...

Like an echo in the forest, life is sweet as honey.

Bring a friend, join the crowd

Watch me bring the fire and set the night alight...

Just like the above lines we have simply best lyrics

With some cheesy line which we would cringe

Some with lovely sound, yet sad lyrics

Some deals with narcissism, self-centeredness and selfishness.

Some deals with motivation, self – confidence, "Dope' as my alarm

Lot of their songs are loaded with love and joy

ARMY's we'll get all that we need

Darkness will fall apart while listening to their music indeed

Love them for who they are

Even though we are far

We'll shower the love and support

'Cause they deserve even more from ARMY's I guess

Sticking together in this journey as an ARMY

That brings scent of memory.

"BORAHAE! !! !!!"

BTS PURPLE STARS

Someone who is sparkly as diamond, someone with priceless talent – RM

Someone who loves his own self and a WWH both physically and mentally – JIN

Someone with beautiful aura and someone who cap (crown) a rap – SUGA

Someone who shares his hope and dazzle with his Award-Winning smile – J HOPE

Someone who depicts all his love for music with his tiny claws – JIMIN

Someone with deep heart and even deeper voice that will melt others heart – V

Someone who cannot be defined with any combination of alphabets, this young one needs different terms to be coined, and is someone who is personified with positivity and love – (Young Kook) JUNG KOOK.

Bangtan Sonyeondan is our asset. The bond we share mentally with the help of their songs are beyond infinity. Forever till night dies, forever till sky falls and forever till stars shines ARMY's will purple you...

SIDDHANTA KHANDELWAL

He is Siddhanta khandelwal he is an engineer and love to write.

BTS

I haven't heard about BTS

but now I have heard about must say

it is good and they are good .

There music and lyrics

are awesome didnt know k pop music is awesome.

TASYA SHRIVASTAVA

Tasya was born on may 26 2002 in shivpuri and is living in gwalior madhya Pradesh .her parents mr.Ashok Shrivastava and mrs. Anita Shrivastava .her biggest supporters & inspiration .Tasya is a student .she follows her passion not only potery but also singing and dancing. I write emotion not alphabet . Tasya Shrivastava @gazal21264 @iamtasyashrivastava

DEAR LOVE JUNGKOOK

Maybe I am just a small part of ur life , but for me you are my whole world , may be I am part of people who want you but you are only person I want . I just know millions girls dying for you and I am nothing special Even knowing everything I can't stop loving you I purple you with my heart ♥ You inspire me you the reason that I smile And You can never see a person who loves u so much And I know you will never know me and my name And that's the sadest part of our love story ..

HIRA TARIQ

Hira Tariq is Pharm-D student indulging in writing her thoughts for worlds to relate with their unspoken feelings. Contact with her through Instagram handle is@_writer_min

BTS

I was alone looking at moon, I was alone looking for cure.

I was disappointed my arts, I was disappointed by new arts.

I was abandoned looking at sun, I was abandoned looking for hope.

I was lonely because of my personality, I was lonely because of my sanity.

I was doubted by my skills, I was doubted by my kin.

I was left out in the crowd, I was left out in the house.

I was charmed by world glories, I was charmed by hidden miseries.

Yet one day I found answers.

One day I was found my gloom, One day I was found by Moon.

One day my art was known, One day my art was Joon.

One day I was preserve by sun, One day I was preserve by Hope.

One day I was accepted by my personality, One day I was accepted by my Agust D.

One day I was praised by my skills, One day I was praised by my Chim.

One I was considered in crowd, One day I was considered by Kim.

One day I was attracted by world glories, One day I was attracted by Jungkookie.

Yet one day I found "My Home",

Yet one day I found "My Bangtan"

© Hira Tariq

TEJASWI.PAPPU

Tejaswi.Pappu is born and brought up in Vishakapatnam, Andhrapradesh . It's,the city of destiny always inspires her to be more creative and thoughtful. she completed M.Tech and doing her phd presently . She is a former educationist, Passionate writer, communication trainer ,Amateur of nature ,wanderlust and avid reader . She is a writer who shares her emotions and thoughts through words, which conveys message in amicable way.

94

OH MY PARADISE, YOU MADE ME REALIZE !

"Who says a dream must be something grand?

Just become anybody We deserve a life

Whatever,big or small,you are you after all."

It was playing in repeated mode while travelling back home.it was the last day of campus interviews. I was almost at the bottom line in every interview even though I bagged top marks.It was all because of my dream which was a fun script for the entire hr bunch. "being girl! Don't fight against gravity! It's difficult to ride on bumpyroads!" they said breaking my wings without even giving a chance to fly.

Interviews always start with aptitude test,with was least important in after levels.i just passed with boarder marks.nevertheless I was out in the next rounds.my dream was so peculiar,that make me loose the confidence. As like before that interview ended with wack results. Few free advices and never-walked-in-that-path suggestions were shared without even asking. 'When mood is good we focus on the music,incase the day was shitty we try to understand deep meaning of lyrics!' Those lines from the BTS album the paradise gave a little hope that not every dream was big,yes not every dream was big when seen in parameters quantity -money, status.

WINNING MOMENT

Not even idea was wowish , sometimes just means to give smile .

Not every moment was winning one,sometimes falling down and breaking bones save a billion words of memories.

When I reached home after a big wack day, I saw a letter waiting for me on the table. Since my both parents were working,no one checked the lying unanswered message carrying paper.

"We are happy to hear your idea. So happy to be part of our team.we are looking forward to work together in coming days!"

Regards &congrats

Team RedCross

Those few words turned my day upside down.my little idea,which was never appreciated by anyone finally got where it had to place.Sometimes few incidents creates a big impact in life.those lyrics sung by jungkoon took the award winning moment then.

ASMA GHALIB

She is Asma ghalib. Self love isn't selfish its important ?

JUNGBOOK AS A BOYFRIEND

I'm going to be the happiest person on earth if he met his lifepartner that lucky girl will be the one for him. Yes ,I will support him and love him for sure I will never forget him..I Actually crossed everything he said but still I'm a lover and will be the lover .I mean I loved Jungkook as a boyfriend and husband .....how can't I when he is the one person whom I fell for in first place . But when it comes to Jungkook's happiness I can let him go .As an Idol he is more then fine and perfect in everything he does .As a Fan I'm very proud to be called ARMY . I want to meet him ones in my Life time as every fan of JK is a world to him .I'm also a world of him so I'm trying my best to control my emotions for him to be happy in my life as he said to be . I know he will never be mine but I know one thing he will never disappoint me and I really mean it .

BTS IDOLS

Every idol have a right to live their own lifes so no looking back they will always be in our hearts as idols if its BTS ,EXO or other groups .after all they will live a happy life with the memories .

If they disband it doesn't mean that they aren't idols anymore they will be but not as a group but as a individual idols.i hope we all live as one as the idols .If we can't meet the idols it doesn't mean we are not fans it means we are special .after all everyone live under the same sky.

They also have a life they love us army. If they are happy we should also be happy like they are .i want them to be happy with whom they are and I want they all should date after all they are adults and have their own lifes and live like normal people how we live .army need to understand that we don't own their lives .they are also humans .

T. KARTHIKEYAN

He is a childhood painter in the field of poet who tries to paint the fountain of his soul in poetry

MY LOVE IS TRUE

My heart is beating,

Even my beloved's projectile eyes attacked it harshly,

But one thing,

There is no other powerful guns can't make a simple abrasion
on it!

Because..,

My love is true?

100 PERCENT

I fervour the Lord 100 percentage,

But I'm not believe in the prayer,

Because,

God is not God,

When he punished someone for not devoting him,

God is not God,

When he not punished the culprit for keep on devoting him!

"What I will say to all my loved ones"

Dharma alone a strongest bullet proof, whoever and whatever can't ruin!

JUHI PUSADKAR

She is 20 yrs old girl from Maharashtra.She loves to write and dance.. Her priority is her self respect... She believes in self

confidence and faith..

BULLETPROOF BOY SCOUTS...

The seven Angels from South Korea ruling the whole world. Telling whole world to love themselves. The seven normal boys being chaotic, talented , funny, cute, handsome, and humble helping the whole world fight with the depressions.

They have save life of many people around them aware of it they never take credits or feel over proud on their achievements. They had started from nothing and now are the one with almost everything. Struggle and hard work are very small words for them and their achievements.

They are the best examples of true friendship, they had shown me that, " No matter how much different age you have, if you know what real friends means then you can maintain friendship until death and people will remember your friendship forever."

They are not girls, they are not fake, they are not with only girls stans but they are the one who really knows how to maintain their talents and to make people happy. Inspite of having different language they knows teaching people about life, struggle, knowledge, and many more are the most important.

That's reason they are known as "Bullet proofs' and they have the best people to protect them known as "The BTS army" !!

BANGTAN SONYEONDAN !

It's the story of Rainbow Light

Begins with the Purple Side,

Learning from the Seven Light

Living like a Dynamite,

Making families Worldwide

Letting our Depression Fights,

Creating Memories Together

Maintaining our Friendship Eternal,

Searching for the Magic Shop

Learning not to Lose Hope,

Smiling for the Affection

Staying with the Reflection,

Teasing our friend as an Alien

Starting to love the Universe,

Telling us to be Fine

By showing us the Spring Day Night,

Choosing between the Blue and Grey

Let's make the Gold Stay,

Hoping to take a Run

By remembering something is Yet To Come ,

Wishing that Life Goes On

With the Bulletproof BANGTAN SONYEONDAN!!!

CHAPTER TWENTY-FOUR

DR.MAHIMA SINGH

Introduction of Dr. Mahima Singh
Born and brought up in Lucknow, she is a graduate from IT
College, has a Masters (in Geography and English Literature)
from Kanpur University and a Ph.D in Geography. She
participates in many seminars and is a woman of socially active
personality, who is associated with many social works. She is

also a founding member of Care for Nature Organization.

BTS

BTS a.k.a BANGTAN TV is a South Korean Band which gained popularity globally during 2018 and 2019.

Their members are Jin Suga, J-Hope, RM, Jimin and the most popular of them all Jungkook.

The 3 most popular songs composed by them currently are Dynamite, Boy with Luv and DNA.

Their first album which gained popularity was 2 Cool 4 School in 2013.

In 2017, they crossed into the global music market and led the Korean wave to the United States of America.

They became the first Korean ensemble to receive a Gold certification from the Recording Industry Association of America (RIAA) for their song Mic Drop.

BTS became one of the fed bands since The Beatles to chart 4 US number one albums in less than 2 years.

The group's accolades include multiple American Music Awards, Billboard Music Awards, Golden Disc Awards, and nominations for five Grammy Awards.

Apart from music, they have addressed three sessions of the United Nations General Assembly and partnered with UNICEF in 2017 to establish the Love Myself anti-violence campaign.

On June 14, 2022, the band announced pause in music activities to enable the members to complete their mandatory military service for South Korea with a reunion planned for 2025. Oldest

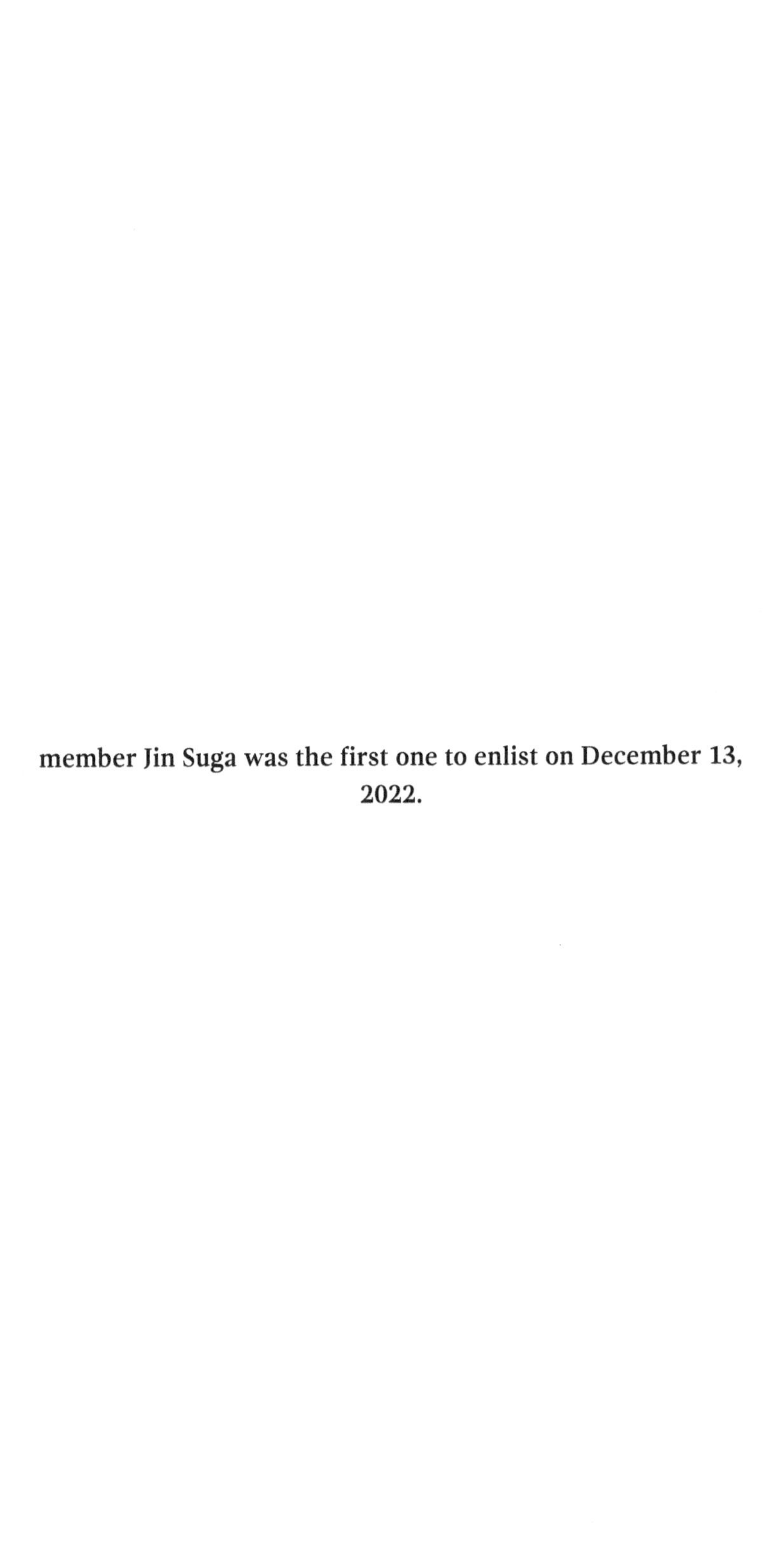

member Jin Suga was the first one to enlist on December 13, 2022.

BTS A BAND

A band that's on top of every chart.

BTS,

A band that stole everyone's heart.

There is nothing as popular as their dance,

Not even the Eiffel Tower of France.

They rock my world with their voice,

When it comes to songs I have no other choice.

They are the world's most successful band,

But also the one making a happier land.

I listen to music all the time but a band like them I have never heard,

BTS is truly one of the best bands in the world.

Copyright ©?

Dr. Mahima Singh

Lucknow, Uttar Pradesh

CHAPTER TWENTY-FIVE

SAKINA K LALANI

Name: sakina komail abbas lalani

Age: 17
Recidence: mahuva, bhavnagar, gujarat, India
E-mail address: <u>sakinalalani110@gmail.com</u>
Ambition: app developer
Passion: writing

BTS JOKES

Seokji's joke and fear in kitchen with his future wife.

I am in kitchen with Jin...actually we both cook together as the maids are out for a month because of some reason...

Sara: *trying to open a can of sprite* oh the can opener's broken

Jin: so it's a can't opener?

Sara: why did I marry you

Jin: because I am WORLD WIDE HANDSOME YOU KNOW?...

both wheezing in disbelief

After sometime

Sara: what are you doing?

Jin: [standing on a chair] I live in house too you know I can stand wherever I want thank you very much

Sara: where's the cockroach

Jin: I-t's u-nder the ta-ble please get It for me please Sara!!...

Sara: ok ok...

She murdered the cockroach with Jin's pink slipper...and started laughing

Sara: you get down...Mr WORLD WIDE SCARED PERSON...

Jin: yaahhh...

....

Jin: I wasn't that scared tho- I could have do that but I wasn't
able to find my slippers...

Sara: seriously they were right in front of you...

Jin: let that be...

SEOKJIN IN FUTURE

Seokjin in future with his wife daughter and son

Jin: wow...you're looking WORLD WIDE
BEAUTIFUL...*Whispering*

Areum: thanks appa...hehe...

Sara: Appa's pet...

Areum: Amma!! Appa tell her...not to tease *whining like a kid*

Jin: yaah don't...

Sara: it's even now...

I kissed ye Joon's forhead...

He kissed Areum's forhead

Jin: time flew so fast!

Sara: hmm...kids get ready you don't wanna go college Areum...

Areum: ready Amma...

Sara: your project...and joonie your assignment...

Ye joon: thank for reminding I would get detention if I forgot to
take it....thanks Amma..

Jin: drink it hAreum: Appa I'm full...

Jin: just two sips...1 for appa and other for WWH..

Sara: waah...what an appa...always admire himself...

Jin: you know who is the most powerful father?

Ye joon: no not again!!!!

Jin: godfather...

Sara: oh god...why did I marry you...

Jin: I told you already because I'm WWH...

Areum: mom appa is right...I agree because I'm WWB...

Ye joon: coz I'm WWB *Mocking her*

Areum: yah you brat I'll kill you!

Ye joon: never...bralalalala....

Areum: yaaah stop!!

Ye joon: yaaaaahh never...

Areun: yah you shut up!

Ye joon: you shut up!

Jin: *angry rap* yaaaaaaaaaah you shut up stop fighting you monkeys your tensing me and your mom and making my house a zoo...fighting like cat and dog... if you wanna fight please go to the zoo it's not a fish market or a taxi stand or a bus stand try to understand please act Normal...don't be nuts you coconut heads...if you want to fight like Tom and Jerry go to the zoo...can't you be like siblings for just sometime you ungrateful spoiled brats!!! Just shhhhhhhhhh!!!! Or I will kick you out of my house!!! (Out of Breath) *Awkward silence*

SHRADDHA SORI

She is shraddha Sori from Chhattisgarh, India. She had recently graduated from the Biotechnology stream and preparing herself to get closer to his dream. She love spending time with his family and friends. Reading manga, drawing and painting in his free time is the best part of her Day. She has an interest in learning and doing new things. She likes gardening too, as her craze for succulents is growing day by day, especially cacti. She hope you can forgive me for her mistake and enjoy reading her writing.

BOY WITH LOVE

They are the Boy with Luv

Comes from the place you love,

Taught us to stop blaming ourself

Showed the sparkling way to love yourself.

On the stormy days of the month

You showed all the sky in blue and grey,

The pain within me is fading away

I can see the burning fire on my way.

Waiting for spring to come again

So we can see together blooming flower again,

Like a burning Asteroid, you are here again

Just hold me tight so I can't lose myself again.

Giving me wings so I can fly over

Showing the path to shine forever,

When I fall you are here to hold me up

The boxy smile of yours can cheer me up.

It's a relief because you are here

Blocking my way to disappear,

Never imagined this could be real

You all seven promise to be with me together.

BOND

There is a strange connection

Between you and me,

How can I show it to other

Because this can't be seen.

Bounded to struggle

Something we want to achieve,

Faced the criticism and

Wronged the hypocrites.

Met in the place

Which is called Big Hit,

Rocked the whole world

With No More Dream.

We're Bulletproof Boy Scouts

With a gigantic wave of ARMY,

If someone messes with us

We shower the lighting stick.

This is a bouquet of

Seven different flowers,

Four are the old ones

Three are still minor.

When this flower comes together

We sing the song

Kim Namjoon, Kim Seokjin

Min Yoongi, Jung Hosek

Park Jimin, Kim Taehyung

Jeon Jungkook BTS.

CHAPTER TWENTY-SEVEN

CLOCHARD

One of the versatile & creative writers , Clochard (Firdous Alam) was born in 1998 , 11th may in northeastern region of india. He is well known for his unique mixture of different literary genres and devices . Most of his writings are associated with both the fiction and non-fiction narrative and he himself loves to write in "free-style".

BTS FROM SOUTH KOREA

In the history of global boy band music, the popularity of The Jackson 5, Backstreet Boys, NSYNC, BTS and ONE DIRECTION will always be unparalleled. Their concerts can be considered as Induced seismicity.

Among all the boy bands, BTS is the one that has made the entire world to copy their Designs of clothes. The boys have started to copy even the hairstyles of this famous band and most significant fact is that each and every girl in this era wants a boyfriend either from BTS or from South Korea.